T0162640

Whoosh

Whoosh

B. J. BUHROW

WHOOSH

iUniverse books may be ordered through booksellers or by contacting:

iUniverse
1663 Liberty Drive
Bloomington, IN 47403
www.iuniverse.com
1-800-Authors (1-800-288-4677)

ISBN: 978-1-4917-8993-3 (sc)
ISBN: 978-1-4917-9040-3 (e)

Print information available on the last page.

iUniverse rev. date: 02/11/2016

This book is dedicated to David, my muse,
my editor and my best friend.

Acknowledgements

Boulevard: Moon

The Bijou Review: Sucker Punch

Contents

Animals

Not Quite Angels

Animals

August

Last night was the sturgeon moon.
It was rosy
as an almost healed bashed-in eye.
When my own eye was swollen
and sealed
I looked about as captivating
as a sturgeon
which is a primeval hideous fish
caught for bragging rights and its roe.
The white people up north
don't catch sturgeon under this moon
with its promises.
They wait until winter.
What can you say about ice fishing
except that it is staring
into a round of black water cut
inside a cold hut.
When my hurt eye opened it felt
like a tired flower at the end of summer.
What can you say about fighting
except that it is never fair.

Wren

I dredge up the taste
of the last drink I had
four years ago.
Cheap vodka like choking on coins.

Even after I stopped
my wife left me.
The house is all mine
with its cracked pipes and buckled floors.

These are things I could fix
now that my hands are steady.
But I still lack a decent hammer
or a wrench and a wren

is visiting a branch outside the door.
Her singing is supposed to bring good luck.
She doesn't sing because she is thirsty
as a small brown rag knocked around by the wind.

Midnight Sun

I am hallucinating that you love me
under the midnight sun of Alaska
where the daylight sifts through the trees like sand.
Beside the luminous dunes
I have pitched a tent made of blue material
thin as a whistle which even wolves can't hear.

Cupid is a baby with a birth defect of wings.
Through the flap of my door I see many things in flight.
The snowy owl which is vicious enough
to eat other owls when its prey is scarce
the fireflies flirting away their brittle lives
during the almost never ending dusk.

Certainly I can have the companionship
of the many drunks
in the many bars which close only to clean up a bit
an hour before opening again
to the next whoosh of the wave of drunks.
But they are people who fall down or evaporate.

They are much more impermanent than you my love
speaking to me in such a melodious and foreign language.
I am not sleep-deprived
because I deprive sleep of myself.
It is sleep that is lonely and waiting for summer to end
and longing for the most lasting nights.

Badly Painted Birds

I don't do drugs anymore.
I go to a meeting every week and in the background
is a painting of birds
badly painted birds
like white blobs of tissue torpedoes.
The bird painting is a distraction
from the difficult iffy work of recovery.
It makes me feel like a resentful cheerleader
the one who buckled
on the bottom of the pyramid.
I can barely follow the girl who is weeping
over her brother who never talks
and will never get better because you have to talk
in the way mold gives birth to penicillin.
Thank you Sir Alexander Fleming
for thinking so hard.
Most of us in this room were prone
to infection
due to lacerations on wrists and stranded needles.
Before us,
people died from the prick of a thorn on a rose.
Oh I am trying not to be a hater
of people who should never try to paint birds
or of birds themselves
with wings like hope
their feathers stroking the dangerous air.

Sheepskin Heart

Flora I saw you at the county fair.
There were prairies of salt between us.
I wanted to cross them in a red tractor.

The sheep were penned in wire,
frantic to eat the straw at their feet.
There were connoisseurs of tractors

who talked tractor and mounted polished
gears in their dens.
There were judges of pies and cakes

and a judge of high school bands
who played the triangle
and choose his winner based on shame.

I bought you this small scrap of sheepskin.
It cost sixty five cents
which was not the measure of my esteem for you

because I spent a good amount of time
braving the witch eyes of the wool hut owner
sorting through baskets of shapeless pieces

until I found the only one
cut out like a pretty soft heart
not the kind of heart beating inside an animal.

Falsies

I am painting the walls of the Boom Boom Room.
When the ladies come in
they look like baskets of clothes on wash day.
I am an old guy.
They like to tease me the way you tease
a blister with a needle.
I remember falsies and when a girl
went naked she was real and bashful.
Now these dancers have to be bare from the get-go
so they have implants
and some of them look so stretched
it must hurt.
They have voices like tinny bells and bad tempers.
You can't dodge what's under your skin.
I remember the story about the gingerbread boy
who ran away and got snapped up by a wolf.
That was a warning to keep
to my brush and drop cloth and not dream.
Retired friends come from out of town and nudge
me about this job.
And I pretend that exotic is the right word.

Again

Each disheveled minute of work
brought her closer to being fired again

and when she was finally fired again
the face of her boss blanched at her careless fury

she was unafraid to walk home in the dark
under the ever more delirious moon

ingratiated herself with the tiny bats traipsing tree to tree
telling them in a voice higher than sonar

how she had won out against the normalcy of daylight again
although it was a struggle

like a shark pulled out of the sea twisting on a rope and hook
still biting at the weekend fisherman posing by his trophy.

Mice

The woman who owns this house doesn't mind us much.
The neighbors think her house is a crime
because it is full of holes, but really.
We can cram ourselves through the smallest crack.
Loose shingles are mired in the rice paddy
of her lawn, but when we take a vacation
from the attic, the yard feels safe as tourist America.
When she gets lectured she answers to "Maria"
but that's not her name.
She leaves behind so many crumbs
that we don't need to harm the wires or insulation.
She converses politely with our skittering in the walls,
we can appear before her in natural light
because she is always daydreaming, and she is
our dream hostess. But when she really sleeps,
she will often stiffen and her eyes open
like unaimed cameras.
And we know what this means, having been stalked
by all-knowing owls, by heat-seeking snakes.

Naming Names

The man's face was a sling for a grin.
He smelled of damp wool although it hadn't rained yet.
He worked at the protectorate.
He asked for papers in this roofless place
where every name painted crudely on the walls
was vilified by other words.
He whistled a crumb of a melody.
Beggars can't be choosers little bird he said.
Would I like a drink.
Would I like a cigarette.
I could see the sky was patient as a landmine
and that the former truths no longer existed.

Pigs

Experimental pigs in the laboratory
alike and alike
but particular
as the scientists in their white coats
each thinking their own thoughts
like damp straw perfumed with ammonia.

Exhibition pigs at the state fair
in the concrete barns
descending into sleep
slabs of breathing
living on family farms in slow blunt motion
under all the blue ribbons of the sea.

Wild pigs achieving varmint status
in the woods of Arkansas.
Tusks and snuffling needful of a shotgun.
They get shot down but still
advance to legend status
and star in quickie TV horror movies

Pet pigs
small and pink and clean and privileged
smarter than dogs
sweeter than cats
waddling through the living room
like a teachable moment.

Perverts and Pandas

Sometimes compassion trips on its own feet.
Sometimes mercy just needs to use the bathroom.

When the journalist traps the perverts on TV
the perverts look bashful and say, "Oops"

but they yelp when the officers aim low with their nightsticks.
Pain is the beginning of understanding.

When pandas hump in a movie it's not obscene
because they look like huge toys accidentally paired by children.

And children are so innocent they can be raised
by dogs, by wolves, even by chickens.

Some of the perverts look like they've been treated
by a dentist from the end of the world.

Nothing says "freak" like missing teeth.
Not surprisingly, many perverts are virgins.

Pandas can't stand other pandas.
They like to eat, sleep and defecate in solitary,

too stubborn to take a one minute break
from revulsion to screw and save their species.

Pandas make us irrationally happy
while the apologies of perverts just creep us out.

Sometimes absolution falls off a bar stool.
Sometimes a savior is subpoenaed but doesn't show up.

Sucker Punch

When the armored tank was hit, your buddy
went from slamming banging wolfwhistles
to take my pulse, take my breath
something fuzzy going on hey hey in your head
the desert lit up like a concession stand for Christmas
in the dust storm. Your sergeant talks
like a caveman's professor, hell, everyone's on pills,
waiting to soap up in Tehran, everyone's safety-pinned
to the promise of home, maraschino cherries in Omaha,
snow, a twenty for every shoeless guy in New York City:

Baby, I'm sorry if I don't write back but I lost the dog.
I just opened the car door and he ran into the night.

The Horses

Psychiatrists used to ask you about your childhood.
Now they ask you about your stress.
Stress is the new childhood.
They prescribe pills and a vacation.
I return to Salt Rock Ranch where I spent a week as a kid
with friends of the family.
The dad was a big kind fat man who wound up
a few years later so skinny from cancer in his coffin
I thought who is this.
The place looks chapped now.
The air is dry as sticks.
The owners added televisions to every room
because they had to.
People need white noise to sleep.
And the guests don't want to bale hay or feed the horses.
They are afraid of horse bites.
Horses have big square vegetarian teeth
but can still become skittish
even though they've been ridden down the same
trail their entire lives.
I don't feel safe anywhere, even here.
I pace at night in the hollow glow of my room
and the floor is crumbling,
the grounds are crumbling and in their stalls
the horses with their heads bowed
whinney and shiver.

Natural Disasters

Zeus was a god who preferred
shaking it up in disguise
with mortal women.
Leda was attacked by a white cloud
of feathers that was no swan
but the taste for rape in the shape of a bird

and she sank underneath the *why me*
which is a question like the Mississippi River
overwhelming its banks
depositing cottonmouths inside the walls of residences.
The rescue boats are too small to save everyone
But I believe that you and your bad habits are intact,

that you once again aroused a mess of rubble
really quick and then moved away
with your shakes and a few dollars into a small motel
which looks like it is furnished by
the taste of failure.
You said you tried sober once but just couldn't do it.

I write this small letter to let you know
my new job is sinking between knives in a magician's trunk.
I can't shake an inch out of kilter or I will
taint the trick with my blood.
Then the audience will know what it should never know.
To be truly safe you have to be dead.

Bunny

I met my husband at the county fair
a future farmer of America who breeds
rabbits to be scary

with wide red eyes
and even the kids who have been warned
jump back.

He has a bible-colored head,
and doesn't like me to be taught
by television.

He stares into the black air and lacks sleep.
He doesn't want me to dance
or ask why.

So I don't dance
but I still bump up against the sheetrock of worry
like one of those kidnap girls

who have to keep quiet or else and the or else
has a giant wing span
like the microwaves and other unnatural energies that tamper with the sky.

An Accounting Of Swans

Swans have profiles like Viking ships
The Vikings were expert
pillagers and sailors
because their homeland would not support them
like a bitter wife, a bitter husband
joined in matrimony anything but holy.

They believed in sea monsters because there were sea monsters.
They believed in land because there was land.
But North America was such a disappointment
all slumbering lumber and no gold surfacing
to be fashioned
into objects worthy of kings.

The kings in Europe wisely moved inland
and cultivated swans
for nothing but their beauty.
The graceful gliding of swans on a pond at dusk
made a good end
to the most peevish day.

To harm a swan meant execution.
Who would ask for death in that manner
while death was everywhere.
It was present in the dirty wound made by a nettle
in the flea on a rat
in the eyes of an envious neighbor.

Yet every year the king must have the measure
of the swans,
a number which was the pulse of the steady world
and its ordained divisions.
Because the revolution
was not quite there.
And the terror afterward was still far, far away.

Valentine

I was casting about for valentines
when I hooked a little dragon
with a spiked crocodilian tail and wet wings.
It couldn't breathe fire, just roses of dust.

It could communicate its basic needs by blinking.
After much to and fro
and patience being a virtue I understood
it wanted a meal of crickets.

It was winter and crickets were out of season.
I bought some dear
and brought them back in a closed white carton.
The crickets played on the violins of their bodies a sad song

of brief green grass and the dullness of their prison.
The dragon ate, sloppy with hunger,
and scattered silence across the table which was rock.
Sated it said with its heavy eyelids.

Don't Kill the Dog

I shrug unclaimed corpses into body bags.
I am an employee Monday through Friday.
On weekends I watch horror movies but if
a dog is a character I yell *don't kill the dog*!

Yelling gets me in trouble with the landlord
but the landlord has trouble renting this dump.
So I guess we are even. My mother taught me
don't pick on the little guy, and she taught me vinegar

is the last word in cleaning products
because it touched the lips of Jesus.
After work I douse myself with it watered down.
I use it full strength to swipe

the bathtub and to carve a shine in the windows
and smoky mirrors.
I've tried to clean every inherited
piece of crap knickknack cuffed to a memory.

I used to have a kind of friend
in my parole officer. She let me call her Molly.
She told me she worked hard to be a hard ass
and don't give any kid the middle name Wayne

because she saw that a lot on wanted posters.
She told me where the wrong places were
at the wrong time and called her job stupid.
She checked for marks

on my arms but with an absent mind.
Anyway I only have the blue of bad tattoos
made with a pointed object and prison ink.
Fading but there like all contamination.

The Bruising Skies Lounge

That squat moment when the motorcycles segued
between the yellow lines
in front of the Bruising Skies Lounge
I was in the bar in a corner
not the best place but the only place
to be independent from any connection with parables.
Every patron's face was grinding
like green winds
jacked up on the catastrophic blink
into which honeybees disappear
and all manner of grain and flowers.
There were cigarette burns on the pay phone
that still itched on the wall.
Peoples' tributes to themselves were etched
into muddled surfaces with knives.
Then something animal happened like a U-turn into a trap.
Wretched, wretched was tromping around the interior
until it was just too loud
and then there were several dead and I had cracked bones.
Everyone got interviewed by the cops
about the proportion
of death culture that made up the weight of their minds.
I said seventy-five percent but I was still in the game.
The next day was cottonwoods
all afternoon
showering me with the wishes of their white spores.

Rhinoceros

Look at this picture of a rhinoceros.
The artist has left bare strips of canvas on the body of the animal
maybe to show
the premature death inside it.

The young of a rhinoceros are so ugly
no one films them in documentaries and gives them names
like Tank or Big Sugar.
We don't care how they reach their adulthood,

because they are fields of furrowed hide.
Their eyes are not wide as baby eyes should be
but are almost buried.
And yet they are possible kin to the possible unicorn

with a single magic horn
which is sheared off
after the task of the huge murder is complete.
The poachers leave the entire carcass behind and the jackals

can't even contemplate all that scavenging.
As mammals who mourn
we must be sad about this waste of life but in a distant way, the way
you might fall in love, say, with the Mona Lisa.

Bad For You

Apples absorb pesticides
as they hang ripening on a stem which is reliable
as the stem of an old watch that twists
to make time go on.
Time is bad for you because the cells of the body
are programmed to burst like dud fireworks
Then you become a stick figure
in a drawing made by a typical child.
You were not that type of child and you never listened
to warnings
running out into the raw traffic
growing up abruptly like a blink
with an eyelash in it.
It is bad to give your girl fake jewelry
and be out in the lonesome
like a cowboy riding toward winter
who has to slit open the belly of his animal for a little shelter
to stave off freezing to death
and it is bad for you to be residing under a bridge
slugging back vodka and shouting about
shooting your imaginary horse
very bad to be
keeping awake those who have nothing to lose but sleep.

Frank's Father

Frank's father broke numbers
and got so sloshed on Sundays
that Monday was an illness he couldn't die from

he just looked like unripe strawberries.
His tie was a puzzle to be solved
every damn morning while the sun

stared at him balefully one-eyed like his boss
who keelhauled his employees
through the salty water of the workday.

Frank's father said his life was choking him
and imagine his trying to be a father
and the mystery of hiding eggs

on Easter, hiding them so they could never be found
missing the point and the air smelled
rotten for some time after Jesus

had risen, so no wonder Frank did time and it showed.
And yet, Frank said, you can't quite help loving your dad,
like a horse banks on clover to be sweet.

Frank said, I am a horse
with no visible harness
galloping in a lather by the sea.

Prague

When I go to Eastern Europe
I will carry all my crazy notions about Eastern Europe
in old suitcases
which can stand being kicked around.
Do the people in Eastern Europe
have a spiritual netting of skepticism
which allows them to boost themselves above my belief
that their situation is one part
almost naked blonde women wearing mink
strolling along avenues where castles grimace
and the other part dimmed barn
where a farmer contends with weariness to help a ewe
birth a second lamb?
I will bring all my fine crying for history, all my glass dollars,
all my designs for donations to the moon, and honey
to coax the sun out of hiding
because it will be hiding while I hide my terror of human hawks
perched upon
the most famous magnificent bridge in Prague over the Vltava river
which takes me so many arrogant breaths to cross
that I am whittled to my knees.
What I will carry back home is not a sepia photograph of Eastern Europe
but only my hands raised palms up like a priest
on each flat platform a candy freight train for the children
and for the rest of you
the botched whistles of progress.

Criminal Children

The wildfire feeds on grass
as would a chimera done justice
by a special cartoonist whose brain goes tilt and lights up
like the three dimensional machine formerly
known as pinball.
I was in an institution and it doesn't matter what kind
because in every kind there are artists.
We learn by imitation.
We make a loose fist and draw a mouth on it,
a couple of eyes above the lipstick.
Voila a puppet who speaks and cracks jokes
morbid jokes which veer into babble
about atrocities
then we have to shake shake shake out
all our limbs
as though we are about to run
a marathon in a square of sunlight.

Space Junk

Cowboys
the riders of the bucking
horses and bulls
on the backs of the animals briefly
like soulful posters
stuck to electric poles
during a murdering rain,
I am in China
watching this sort of tribute rodeo.
I don't think my translator
is translating my words correctly.
That is my fault.
I should speak Chinese
as I should never have let you blindfold me
when we went ice skating
at Rockefeller Center.
The figures I traced were obscene
now everywhere I carry with me the ticking suspicion of cruelty.
It is a lonely way to live
as outcast metallic parts of the exploration beyond earth
continue their orbit of earth
singing a crooked technobabble lullaby.

The Dive in the Dark

Oh buddy randomly stuck next to me
on the bar stool and loose as trash,
let me tell you about being the socialite's ghost writer.
I made her sentences wry.
I buried the trapeze artist in the middle of a chapter
in the middle of the book.
I turned her bloated Akita Lassie-like,
always barking like a savior.
I cleaned out her refrigerator because I was under contract.
I can tell you at this time my brain
was all hash and strobe lights.
I lost the glass chin of an artist fast
because I took a drubbing.
I felt like a buoy in low reeds
on a body of water where no swimmer swam
and no boats boated.
I was a cartoon itch on a children's game show.
When the book was done
I drove home to Fort Knoxville
and hogtied my hackneyed self into a binge
so massive it purged July from the calendar
and crippled all future surprises.
That's why I am sincerely yours.
That's why I already know everything about you.

Elephants

The eyes of elephants are erasers
of any history of people being gentle.
Their ears sway like weird runway dresses fashionable
for a single season only.
And their tusks are exquisite sculptures of torches
which illuminate every heavy vandalism
of beautiful churches, synagogues and mosques.
To remind me of my cowardice
in looking away,
I wear the thickest gloves to perform simple actions.
For example, when I peel grapes
or thread a needle or shoplift perfume
which I spray on heavily facing the bedroom mirror.
I hope the elephants will outlast our catastrophic selves.
But in the swords of my bones and the torpedo of my heart
I know this won't happen.
I just heard a family of elephants lies recently dead
and tread on and desecrated on the path
to honor their own dead,
and the vultures are twirling above
like an umbrella in the hot breeze at a resort beside the pool.

You Stole

You were born
under the auspices of Mercury
god of merchandise
and messenger who traveled between a pitiless paradise and earth
with his winged feet, his winged helmet
and his vermillion eyes.
You had an orbital eccentricity that tilted
the bright telescopic cells of suspicion away from you.
Everyone else was an empty lighthouse during a dull spot of weather.
You were small as a flea sleeping inside a dog's ear.
You were fast as a jaguar who abandoned the zoo.
You admitted to me that you liked stealing.
You were naked as snow.
I believed that you were true in this telling
as the temperature announced
by a thermometer that used to be toxic magic liquid stowed inside
a fragile glass stem.

Toes

You had a canvas on your wall of a horse rearing,
a spear in its gut
during a period of old war.
It was afraid, it was not versed in dying.
I was wearing my red stilettos which hurt.
Two middle-aged people were pummeling each other
out in the hall in disagreement
over an injured toe,
who caused the injury, whose pain was heaped upon.
The importance of toes can't be underestimated.
Toes lavish upon people
the ability to walk toward, the ability to walk away.
The fish began to fade inside the aquarium
poisoned by your spilling wine into the water.
They were swimming haltingly
like stitches tearing.
Poor little fishes with no wherewithal to go.

Recovery

In the light of the amber facility
where time is shed
like water off the back of a shaking bird
we are taught the properties of the solvents
we have put into our bodies.
What a hot mess we have made of ourselves.
High fives all around to another day of healing
to following the railroad ties straight into the future
to watching the train resist its derailing.
Still I do not want to be here.
I want to be outside in the dark
walking the black dog between shafts of lighting.

From the Bees

We actually used to like you a lot as a species
you humans
before you laminated yourself in technology
and became blasé about our stings
which were little admonishments not to be so clumsy.
Now you are clumsy
as robots in old robot movies.
The sun is hot,
too hot now, it is a turnoff for sunflowers.
What are you doing, what are you doing
is what we mean when
we beat our wings in the sullen air and disappear.

Honeymoon

In the upper peninsula of Michigan
there are insects called no-see-ums
who bite hard
and there are loons whose cries raise psychic welts.
Secrets make us jangly head and heart.
The fact is there are no fish in this lake.
You are out on the rowboat with your stranded line.
I am on the pier reading a biography of John Wayne Gacy
when, for the first time, I see a snake swim.
Which sickens me.
The fact is all snakes can swim.
A grease paint smile can turn ghastly.
Lonely, I make a little snarl of lies
like tinder which starts the dancing fire
because who are you
and who am I
in this lush forest under the sapphire sky.

The Headless Madonna

Uncle Three Day Weekend is scouting me.
He says he has the eye for talent.
He thinks he is a really good manipulator.
But actually I look much younger than I am.
He stops at the bluefish check cashing store.
He knows a guy.
I make my way through the shoving of the boardwalk.
Welcome to a new party.
The sky is the color of a burnt field.
Someone has molded a small Madonna
all robes and prayer hands
and put her on top of a piling on the pier.
Someone has knocked her head off
with a baseball bat, maybe a brick.
Her face is floating
on a slick of the greenish sea.
Uncle comes out with his paper fan of money.
We walk and he is talking but I don't listen.
I look down like I am shy.
At the base of my foot is a dove with the coo kicked out of it.
And the flies are busy
laying many gross offspring
underneath the stiff shelter of its stilled wings.

Not Quite Angels

Babysitter to the Vampires

Like other kids they want the fast food experience
if just to throw French fries at each other
and bully the hamburgers.
The workers are not paid enough to notice
anything strange.

I have to clean up the messes they leave behind
usually the drained bodies of mean teachers
who don't empathize with their disability
which is actually a disease in the medical literature
afflicting children who can only play outside
on very dark nights
because even starlight hurts.

I think this is sad but my charges
don't know what sad is.
When I drive them with their coffins in my van down the interstate
there is a lot of road kill
mostly raccoons which are supposed to be wily
but vaingloriously refused
to act second class when the territory turned human.

It is hard to feel affection for beings
who have no love for other
than their own kind
and even with their own kind love is a stretch,

but when the children are asleep I do have the urge
to brush back
the wild silk of their hair from their pallid foreheads.
They don't look peaceful when they rest.
But they do look gratified.

Black Dust

Something is happening
like breathing in black dust
that comes when fixing car parts.
I don't know much about cars.
Donnie does but he's still in prison.
I give the dog her pills, I forget to take my own.
I am supposed to think about just this day.
And cut it like a flower.
Smell the roses.
But I keep thinking about the time I was pregnant
big as a cow
and on TV there was this baby
with an arm blown off by a landmine
lying on its back in bandages
with a look of no expectation in its eyes.
I wept and wailed enough for an entire war.
I have used up my tears.
I have moved home with my mother.
We live above the A+R Garage.
Sometimes I stand like an animal out in a field.
The sky bears down.
It shows the silver lining
which turns out to be the shaking and shining leaves
of those kind of trees I never learned what kind.

A Geography Lesson

Vancouver is the serial killer capitol of Canada.

The State of Alaska is the feeling of anticipation
when you're waiting for someone to show up at your home
and you keep going outside to see if they are there yet.

Dakota is where many people with faces
badly in need of a fist
observe that there are many faces in need of a fist.

In Asheville, the act of gazing vacantly into the distance without
thinking has its own word and that word is Boketto.

Ontario is a constant of chattering teeth.

Virginia is the place to tenderly run your fingers through
your lover's extravagant hair.

New York City is the point of origin of the practice of being unfaithful
and then trying to revive
a nonviable relationship like reheating cabbage.

In Haiti knowing peace is not just a good dream it is an amazing dream.

Miami is strange.

In Chicago the gunshots are as common as sandwiches.

Chinatown is a sculpture of random silver letters
soldered into the elusive shape
of a philosopher contemplating fireworks which illuminate the greatness
of a great wall.

Each of the Great Lakes has its own blue
underneath the waves that crest white
then fall
in the shades of ink
used to write
controversial and irresistible stories.

To Read

I had a job down in Georgia
in the fifties
pulling bark off trees with my bare hands.
The forests in the south are nasty
with bugs, snakes.
Look at my back all humped with the wrong muscles.
Look at my fingers going crooked at the joints.
The pay was nothing but a little pay.
I drank it up.
I bought my faithless girl bangles.
They never did tell me what the point was.
If they were saving the trees
the way you tear off burned skin
so the good skin underneath can show
or if they were making the trees die off a little faster.
I didn't have any choice back then no sir.
So I ended up here where they give you a meal and a cot
and kick you out at sunup.
All day I have to figure out what to do.
I can't read on paper.
All I can read is wood
before it is ground up, mashed, spit out all bleached
and soft enough
to take in what you have to tell.

Off the Coast of Newfoundland

The plane swooned like an assaulted angel
into the freezing Atlantic.
Everyone on board died.
Everyone dies.
When people say they don't expect a miracle,
they do, in fact, expect a miracle.

A flashy preacher said Jesus dressed well.
I remove stains in the back of a dry cleaners.
The chemicals make me drowsy.
Here is a wedding gown transparent as make-believe.
Here is a winter coat with buttons missing.

The cold will catch up, the wearer will surrender
like the cod my ancestors trapped
off the banks in baskets. In those days
the schools of fish were so thick
you could almost walk on their flesh into the sea.

My "crazy" aunt taught me to swim.
She was legally blind and a good friend to the water.
I used to pray for her eyes to get better
like a dog barking at a falling maple leaf.

The crash was big news for a day.
Once I wanted to be famous but now I don't.
Winners of the lottery piss it all away.
Money is pulp and then it's paper
and then it's sodden again in the pockets of the drowned.

Gravy

After school and majorette practice
I work at a nursing home.
I help feed the invalids.
Chicken salad sandwiches, canned corn, apple slices
everything is served with gravy
in a frilly paper cup.
Gravy helps the food slip down the throats
of the difficult swallowers,
the ones with paralyzed muscles or the ones who just don't want to eat.
I want to eat all the time,
but my uniform has limits, ha ha,
and I can't use a crow bar.
Discipline and discipline because I am the good kid
with smarts, and my sister
is the bad kid who is pretty with no future.
I wipe globs of crumbs off cheeks and chins.
I never flinch, like that time at the parade
when I bonked myself on the head with my baton
and saw angels diving around wearing utility belts
and glitter sandals, then slipped into the dark
which was all so nice I never told anyone,
but just came to so the audience clapped extra hard
as I stood up and twirled for all I was worth.

The Voice of Love

This is the voice of love
which sounds a lot like the voice of worry.
I have written you a constellation of letters.
I wrote one on rope.
I wrote one after a riotous fight among the elms
in the holding tank
while felons watched.
I wrote one on a litmus strip and one
on my torn shirt.
I waited to hear back from you and nothing.
I felt like the fracture in the cornerstone
of a building already riddled with cubicles and it was only Tuesday.
So I prayed to St. Thorazine
patron saint of acid trips gone wrong at proms in the early seventies,
and to Loki the Norse god
a bad god among badder gods
who controls all the luck in the world.
Bring me a message
on sheet lightning if you have to
on a crust of bread stolen from a veteran beggar,
as a piece of the plaintive protests of seawater held hostage
in copper pipes.

I was so desperate for one sweet
word from you that I put on a full body bunny suit
and volunteered full of candy at a kindergarten before spring broke
but I couldn't see through the slits-for-eyes
and I asked to exchange heads with the other fellows,
one was an old man with the shakes and one was a young man
who bristled with piercings and neither complied.
I experienced sweat and tears but not blood
and for that I am thankful but
my longing for you is becoming pitiful and hideous
as a tangle of snakes.
I would accept an echo of an echo of an echo
of your blessing
until the tree of life is rotten at every root
then we die
and your answer or the aching lack of an answer will
not matter at all.

Escapee

When I was in jail
this big looming guy
wanted me to be his blue eyed bitch.

I did not requite this,
I spun away like a skinny compass needle
among the cells, on the stairs.

For a while I managed.
Then one day on the rec field
I was surprised by him and the beat down of his buddies.

Gravity prevailed.
When I came to
I was alone and the sky was the ceiling.

Despite my whacked brain
I realized that by being left behind lying on the ground
I was an escapee.

I was outside the orbit of the guards.
I felt a Martian fever for the guards, everything
the guards failed to do or see was just

a pulse of dust
which could in no way be recorded.
So I knocked at the door and begged

to be locked up again.
I was lucky and didn't get more time.
I did the rest of my sentence and my time ended.

Jail taught me to be a goddamn citizen
on the right side of the day when the sun shines
and nobody's honey inside the night.

Lake Superior

I was seven and a half years sober
when I went on a business trip to California.
No one was watching me.
I stopped at a bar, threw back a few
and met up with these guys who suggested
going to a club. By then, I was oiled up for anything.
The driver turned out to be a whack job
and at a hundred miles an hour blew two tires.
There was only one spare, and questionable characters
began to slink out of alleyways and I ran
and slept in the underbrush by a freeway ramp.
When I woke up I looked like I'd slept
in the underbrush by a freeway ramp.
Did you know that the frontal lobe of your brain
is thinking of everything all the time?
I want to comb my hair, I want to fuck the bartender,
I hate the rain, my boss is a moron.
But now I'm picturing Lake Superior,
only Lake Superior.
When I was a kid I dabbled in the shallows
so clean and cold you could pick out
the exact quartz-veined rock you wanted.
But that lake can go crazy.
It contains shipwrecks galore and the bones of the sailors.
I bet some of those crewmen died in the dark drunk.
I fractured my big toe on that night in California.
Nothing could be done but limp and let it heal.

The Wraith of Mata Hari

The tree was a silver maple,
strangling the sky with its leaves,
killing the lawn with it roots like poisonous broaches.
It was growing bolder surreptitiously
It grew five feet inside a week I swear.
Its canopy was a parasol which made the sun weak as milk.
Its branches were surveilling the house.
I had to plan the assassination sealed in the dark
of the bathroom in the basement by
the small light of a candle.
Not grand at all, not like the jungle and the blasts of defoliant
which illuminated the roar of the tigers
tigers which the boys in camouflage swore were there.
No, all I needed was one desperate Hungarian
with third hand equipment
and a car full of waiting children crying wolf wolf
in their new language.
Only well-cared for children cry wolf
the abused ones are silent
as the aftermath of the buzzsaw, the wood chipper, the ringing
chop chop of the axe.
Then my backyard was quiet, almost too quiet,
with another depression in the ground, no grave.

Five Sisters

I am the hearse driver.
I take myself seriously.
I show up at x date x time.
I proceed through the intersection with slow flags.
I am trusted.
Even if my arm is broken I can change a flat tire.
I know the territory.
I like to eat dinner at a Chinese restaurant
where five sisters work under the ordained direction
of their oldest brother
who is a real dragon and docks wages
when someone runs out on the check.
My sympathy has been honed by my job.
I am a good tipper.
Each sister reminds me of a different sort of grief
while they wilt in the heat of the kitchen
while they smile like silk flowers.

Purpose

When you boarded the rocket to Mars
you were peaceful.
You were not blowing through a red light.
Your shirt was not on fire.
The gesture you made toward me meant
I was being hired to remember you
and my only duty was to match my manner of breathing to the tides.
You thought I could do this.
I thought of sitting with you in the parking lot
outside the white wooden church
where the Presbyterian children of miners brought over from Wales
sang hymns
even though the red granite quarry had long been flooded
and made a dump for rusty appliances
beside a sign that said swim at your own risk
and how you dove in to bring up treasures but after
they dried out the glisten was gone and they were not treasures.
When this quest came along
you didn't have to think fast or about
apples or oranges
it was exit only to discover life elsewhere.
Your purpose never subsides
like the miles of scarlet sunrise always circling the earth.
Your hope is so terrible you will love
whatever you find,
whether it is a corrosive seraph or a liquid beast.

The Tubercular Bride

She was a lacemaker.
People wondered where she received her delicate training.
The butcher saw her pallor and thinness
and took that for comeliness
and vowed she would never lack for a meal,
in fact she would grow fatter
to bear his weight, to bear his children.
But not like a sow on her side
in the straw heaving to breathe.
Never.
In return she would refine him with a fancy collar.
He was besotted with the idea
of climbing the ladder of society.
The small city needed him for sustenance.
The small city did not need her but wanted her
for betterment in the thoughts of the other small cities.
She was a luxury.
The wife-to-be coughed the night away
awake at the window
thinking how many stars there are tatted on the black sky
and how will I find my way to the altar without fainting.
She was smart, that one, and a liar
consenting to the wedding day during the winter
when her appearance conspired with the snow.

The Interview

I interviewed for the job.
I was at the center of the unfolding.
Was I an arrow?
Did I know everything?

They had a point of view let's just say that.
Which had a frostbite feel to it.
The judgment of the bells and the stars.
They were involved.

They were in my head.
I couldn't focus
there was a drill going after the bolts on the bridge
and the everlasting semi in a vision of rush.

I had no expectations, I was guessing, guessing.
The impression of many crows
followed me home
past the cinderblock, past the detour, past the eastern slopes of the
cutthroat mountains.

Eurydice

You were singing about love on our wedding day
when I danced on vipers.

After I died you sang about love
to the wife of the god of hell and she wept tears

as red as pomegranate seeds.
The devil knows the science of candy

which is all spinning and rocks.
He knew about your doubting nature.

I followed you like a burr
stuck to the unraveling threads of your human clothing

while trudging up the slope of shadows.
I was this close to being real again

when you broke your promise
and looked back

and the sour excitement of bats dragging me down in their beating net
drowned out the music of your little sorry.

Everyone says, poor Orpheus who braved Cerberus and Lethe.
Poor Orpheus who lost his beloved twice.

Poor Orpheus torn to pieces by drunken marauding women in the forest.
I continue to linger here where you consigned me,

in a place without dawn, without pleasure. I am voiceless.
But I would ask why

was my negligent husband rewarded with a new body of diamonds
which dazzle in the sky?

Where Are You?

The church bells sound
like a necklace with a broken clasp
in this rainy night.
I am drinking the last of the beer.
I am telling the dog, quiet champ.
He is astonished by every near sound
that isn't you.
Cars, cats, the wind whipped branches down shore.
The yuk yuk of the guests on the talk shows.
Are you ignoring the porchlight
like a ship plotting its next move in the mist
despite beacons?
Or are you bested?
Fallen and debating yesterday with ravens?

Raise Your Hands

What I learned recently is if you see you are
about to be in a car crash
hold up your hands in the air like you are surrendering.

This is what race car drivers do so their hands
don't get broken on the steering wheel.
This action is not instinctive.

I learned this from a guy with broken hands
who totaled two cars in ten days.
The guy is a trader in scrap metal and the scrap metal markets are
tanking.

He makes a what can you do gesture.
He uses his smarts not his hands.
Hands are essential to the job of racing.

A day or so after I learned this thing,
a race car driver died in a crash on the track.
Each part of him was smashed up and failed.

Which doesn't seem like a good reinforcement about raising your hands
but what I learned is permanent
like a virus that has hypnotized every other cell in my body.

Euphoria

I had one episode of euphoria
and it was good
as golden sheetrock
and the sidewalk was an unmistaken piece of plush.
I had so much charm that people punched me.

I have been plodding on many years without you.
I have regressed in my mood to the middle ages
living on the outskirts of a village
farming mud
I am supposed to be better off without you,

here and thick and slow
shaving fake wood into smaller pieces of fake wood.
If I close my eyes it smells like pine
in a forest where I know I'm not.
They say I am doing especially fine but I know I'm not.

A Bad Place To Cross the River

I saw the mysteries of life
in TV reenactments.
Bleach is the key
to one family member killing another
because random murderers don't clean up.
Sharks have teeth on their skin
to lessen the drag of constantly moving through water
and this discovery was used
to design a better swimsuit so the wearers won
more Olympic medals.

I know what life is.
I watch the forlorn
still keeping up with the dye in their hair,
I see the rich banking savage promises.
Then the wah wah news of the impending end of the world washes away
all the wiring.
How do we discover now?

I had to adopt the fortitude of a pilgrim
although I felt the sheet metal ache of a broke down Winnebago.
I learned you gamble.
You keep going.
You use a bone of unknown origin
to knock down fruit, to fend off and raise bruises.
You stare into the flames you made
to hypnotize yourself
into the willingness to participate in tomorrow,
cranking out rejoicing like a preacher
in a murky suit
drenched up to the knees
at a bad place to cross the river.

Moon

The newest moon has slipped under the earth
to the place where the dead stay.
The dead are always thinking of the living
and make a fresh story about

the moon returning to the sky.
The moon considers this
and rounds a curve and rises again
and the next night provides a fuller sliver of itself

to guide the living
and the tides in their salt travels
and the animals who harvest light
with their eyes.

Dry Sunday

Check out that dumb shit Joe Ball
who got the Sunday DTs
because all the liquor stores are closed by law
and the weathered-to-gray sideboards
of where he stayed last night
emphasize his red T-shirt that faded
to jellyfish pink from the sun
when he lay passed out in the park but wow
now come the shakes and seizures
him acting like a fire
that can't be doused
brain all fistfights and flashing lights
he couldn't remember to stash or ration
for this one day of the week
even though the seven days of the week
are fake
unlike the seasons
or day and night which have natural causes
this day when we remember how
it must have hurt hard for Jesus
who knew when to put his glass down but didn't know
the whole world was coming for him.

Funland

In Funland there is much good clean fun.
There is the cakewalk
which is like musical chairs
without the chairs but the winner gets a cake.
There is a freckle contest and a red hair contest
because beauty is in the eye of the beholder
but the carnies wear dentures by contract
so no one is disturbed by rotten teeth.
Servicemen get a free pass.
If they are in a fugue state or having waking nightmares
someone will assist them
to the balloon dart game and no matter what happens
they are assured of a fuzzy prize.
There are sleigh rides over cotton snow while
birds trill over the loudspeakers.
Birdsong is the only music allowed.
Any visitor has to give a urine sample to be drug-tested.
Bambi is the name of the nurse but she is dressed in scrubs
not a provocative costume.
She can't even wear lip gloss.
I work here and I am not supposed to believe in evolution
or sharing DNA with apes
because apes throw shit around for fun.
I'm not supposed to say the word shit if I must say a word
that word is hooey.
My bosses have a map on the wall of their office
and outside Funland there is just empty space.
And many employees toe the line
because they're so afraid of being part of the part
of the world labeled Here Be Monsters.

Reflex

Your acute startle response will queer it for you in the apocalypse
and by queer I don't mean anything derogatory
derogatory will be your least worry
because the story about sticks and stones breaking your bones
but words not hurting will become true again
as it was true in the decade
of your childhood long before cyberbullying
and yes you did get punched in the nose out of nowhere
you were little and hit by somebody bigger
you touched your face and saw that your fingers
were damp with blood
you emitted a shriek and tried to jump away from your own body
which wore this new garish skin
oh you will be so dead
in the brutal future
triple dog dead
with no compass learning, no ability to scarf down your fear
every tribe withholding every hiding place because you
betray it
like the click clack of the wooden joints of a puppet on strings
in a preset tangle of mythic proportions
unable to maintain
the great vain silence of the hunted who really want to live.

Misspent Youth

I am so glad, Marigold, that I misspent
my youth and with you and your every freckle
which bloomed when the sun shone through
the church glass especially the grass
below the feet of the lamb and your face
was showered with green illumination
and you were sleek as a salamander and I mean
that you were miraculous as a creature who
can grow back a part of your body if some brat
severed it. And how you turned what was sad
such as needles, the prospect of rain, the war news
into stop hurting, trees flourishing, and no news.

In the Distance

My job leads me to
a hangnail town among the blue mountains
beside the boss man river
to a darkened room, wooden unfinished floors
a smoke streaked window
where the moon's orbit was the last vital idea
and the motion of a dog far in the distance
running another animal to the ground
and both the hound and the unnamed terrified animal
are so tired
their legs might shatter
like a crude number system up against the modern notion of physics.

So I come home to you Cynthia
with my research about more poverty.
You are in the back yard
looking like a cherry blossom in the fog.
A photographer from the magazine comes to photograph us,
a husband, a wife, children and leaves behind
one of the lesser photos
the sort of picture an android
might tuck in a wallet
and pull out to display
in case a real human made the puzzling decision
to ask about its family.

Light

So much light!
Like new flocks of canaries each morning in the mine shaft.
Tow truck light.
Helicopter light.
Light like drops of drinkable water
when you are surrounded by sea water,
light like the chatter of dolphins when they are behaving well
and nudge
stranded sailors to safety.
Lighthouse light
in lighthouses that somehow remain unhaunted.
Tendrils of light, punches of light
big square diamonds scintillating on fists made only in self-defense.
Recognition light
behind the blue cataracts curled around
the eyes of old dogs.
Lady light light.
Sir light light light.
Bestowing grace even as we so-called walk
bone grinding on bone above the whole dark world.

Anonymous

A man moves from Michigan to New York City.
He moves from the water of the Great Lakes to the ocean.
He moves from cherry orchards to spindly attempts at trees.
He becomes an artist who is a little famous.

The man has a dog confined in an apartment.
The dog chews on its paw.
The man puts medicine on the sore spot but the dog licks it off.
He puts medicine on the sore but it never gets better.

The man writes anonymous letters to people he knows
who don't know how much they hurt him.
One says *You are a snake swallowing your own tail.*
Another says *You are necessary as Judas.*

The man wakes up in the useless hour before dawn
He rereads the note he posted on the refrigerator.
It says *you said you would be home tomorrow*
and now it's tomorrow and no one is here.

Dead Yet

I am back from Nogales with my cancer pills
which carve my skull into candy.
I have smuggled a few words into America
like siesta and manana,

las estrellas, the stars
and la luna, the moon.
The border streets are so hot that even at night
the wax of the shoeshine stumbles

and some of the chickens drunk with chicken power
which I saw fight
are dead now
but too tough to stew

and I see many an old silver dog pressed into the back
of a flatbed truck,
still accepting hard invitations
to party with fake friends that are wolves.

In this hotel where I have paid for the trouble of sleep,
brothers and sisters I hear you
whispering inside the disguise of the closet
"Is he dead yet?"

I will never be shitfaced enough
and there are not guns enough
addressing me with their stupid O mouths
to ever, ever get me to say.

Calgary

Truth is coming and so is a hard winter.
There are dog bones outside the door.
The sky is a kind of milky froth.
You have to go to the pharmacy, it's a big deal.
An ambulance with its hot red sirens
is counting on you to move over.
You put on your blinker but traffic fails to notice.
That picture your daughter posted from Texas
with your ten year old grandson shouldering a shotgun
grasping a confederate flag,
whoa that was an injury and she knows
a valve in your heart leaks.
A kid in the parking lot pretends to shovel snow
You do a bang up job of waiting in line.
People are talking about frozen bypasses, empty crowds.
You clench a white bag of instructions.
You count your money twice
and you reach your car and force it to start.
Your brain tries attain
a beat inside your chest that is realistic
as the day goes gray in front of you
and you take a little breath and then another little breath.

Bye Felicia

She began late
under the aftershave sky
she was breathing pure plutonium
she exhausted every verb
breach hide borrow
park
Central Park
all the birds in the air
edgy points of reference
and the grinding foxhole of the local economy.
No velvet entitlement there.
She was just one gear in a pick clock
among many dubious artifacts and bad reviews
that could not be repaired by laughter or apologies.
She was shunted toward the aura
of rank red feathers
spilling inside
a car the snow was polished and driving
toward a small corner
of are you bothered by the end of time

Whoosh

I heard the buzzsaw accents of the assailants
before I saw them casting vast nets.
Their sense of heaven was tuned out.
The sunlight was a veil of various dusts

in the red arbors of their salt hearts.
In my fluttering heart I abruptly understood
the meaning of capture and the sad
inevitable aftermath of being adult

which is present at every christening
as a seed is embedded in the formula
for the harvest, as the silver bang

of lightning is crucial for the bringing
of rain. And I did not have the stamina
to know this so I welcomed the haste of the closing in.

Celestial X

I was walking home this morning
After being up all night shimmering with strangers
Still wearing my princess wig and jetliner bracelet
And I felt like that part of the Amazon that has been spoiled by being
discovered
As I watched building after old building being torn down
The rebar singing no baby no
And there goes the tensile strength of the infrastructure
As chips of bricks fell in a hurtful sort of rain.

I felt plaintive as a promised institution of education
Which will never see daylight
So children will continue to have jackal hands and brains like kites
My hallowed vocabulary is so limited
It cannot describe the desolation of my limitations
As angels sure we respond, even intermingle
But the circumference of our ability to actually do anything for you
Has been whittled down
To the size of one tiny bead of sweat.

So today I start my student driving
And what I hear is our wings typically are a great disturbance
Imagine the fire hydrants alone
Colliding with our notable plumage
And becoming liquid columns, geysers really in exquisite states of
collapse
Adults dancing as if the placebo finally worked
Under the murmuration of the lost wisdom of water.

Printed in the United States
By Bookmasters